Who's Right, Addition or Multiplication?

Ann H. Matzke

ROURKE
PUBLISHING
www.rourkepublishing.com

www.rourkepublishing.com

PHOTO CREDITS: Cover: © Willard; Title Page: © Daniel Laflor; Page 3: © Paco Romero; Page 4, 5: © Scowill, dalton00, Willard; Page 6: © Sergii Godovaniuk; Page 7: © Sergii Godovaniuk, Yong hiam Lim; Page 8, 11: © Aliaksey Hintau, Olivier Blondeau; Page 9: © Maxfx; Page 10: © Ron Chapple Studios; Page 12, 13, 14: © RuslanDashinsky; Page 16: © Robyn Mackenzie, Raulo Alejandro Gomez; Page 17: © Danny Smythe, Hans Slegers; Page 18: © kali9; Page 19: © Robyn Mackenzie, Paulo Alejandro Gomez, Danny Smythe; Page 20, 21, 22: © bloodua; Page 23: © Grady Reese;

Edited by Luana Mitten

Cover and Interior design by Teri Intzegian

Library of Congress Cataloging-in-Publication Data

Matzke, Ann
 Who's Right, Addition or Multiplication? / Ann Matzke.
   p. cm. -- (Little World Math)
 Includes bibliographical references and index.
 ISBN 978-1-61741-763-4 (hard cover) (alk. paper)
 ISBN 978-1-61741-965-2 (soft cover)
 Library of Congress Control Number: 2011924810

Rourke Publishing
Printed in the United States of America, North Mankato, Minnesota
060711
060711CL

www.rourkepublishing.com - rourke@rourkepublishing.com
Post Office Box 643328 Vero Beach, Florida 32964

Addition or multiplication, who's right?
Both can help you add when you
use them right.

Use addition when you're adding two or more numbers together.

How much baseball equipment?

$$\begin{array}{r} 2 \\ 2 \\ +3 \\ \hline \end{array}$$

+ + = 7

Use multiplication when you're adding groups of repeating numbers.

How many wheels?

Groups

In each group

$$3 \times 2 = 6$$

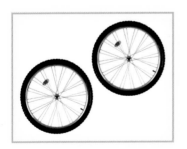 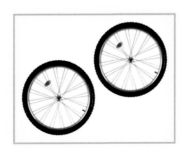 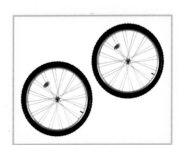

Two pineapples and one orange
equal how much fruit?

Do you add or multiply?

Adding is right!

$$\begin{array}{r} 2 \\ +1 \\ \hline \end{array}$$

 $+$ $= 3$

Five pairs of silly slippers equal
how many silly slippers?

Do you add or multiply?

Multiplying is right!

Groups

In each group

$$5 \times 2$$
$$= 10$$

Three rubber ducks, two beach balls, and three buckets equal how many beach toys?

Do you add or multiply?

Adding is right!

$$\begin{array}{r} 3 \\ 2 \\ +3 \\ \hline \end{array}$$

+ + = 8

Four fishbowls with three goldfish in each bowl equal how many goldfish?

Do you add or multiply?

Multiplying is right!

Groups

In each group

4

x 3

= 12

Addition or multiplication, who's right?
Both can help you add when you
use them right.

Index

Websites

www.ixl.com/math/practice/grade-1-addition-with-pictures-sums-to-10

www.ixl.com/math/practice/grade-1-addition-facts-sums-to-10

www.abcya.com/addition.htm

About the Author

Ann Matzke is a librarian. She lives with her family in the Wild Horse Valley along the old Mormon Trail in Gothenburg, Nebraska. She uses addition and multiplication working in the library. Ann enjoys reading and writing books.